Afghans by the Pound

What is a pound?

If you live in England, a pound is a sum of money.

If you're a dieter, a pound is something very difficult to lose.

If you bake a pound cake, you'll use a pound of sugar, a pound of butter and a pound of flour,

If you're a dog lover, a pound may be where you find your new best friend.

But to a crocheter, a pound is a WHOLE LOT OF YARN!

Those wonderful yarn companies know that when it comes to yarn, crocheters think big! So they've created for us great big balls of yarn that weight a whole pound—sixteen ounces—each.

A pound is a LOT of yarn! A pound will let you make a baby afghan or a small throw; add another pound or two, and the afghans you can make are endless.

These big one-pound skeins come in a wide range of favorite colors, and you will find them addictive, a bit like chocolates!

So get your hook and a few pounds of yarn and start making Afghans by the Pound.

CONTENTS

Carol Wilson Mansfield, Art Director

James Jaeger, Photography

Graphic Solutions inc-chgo, Book Design

Produced by The Creative Partners™

ABBREVIATIONS AND SYMBOLS

sc	single crochet
hdc	half double crochet
dc	double crochet
tr	triple crochet
dtr	double triple crochet
tr tr	triple triple crochet
ch(s)	chain(s)
sl st	slip stitch
beg	begin (ning)
CL(s)	cluster(s)
cont	continue
inc	increase
lp(s)	loop(s)
patt	pattern
prev	previous
rem	remaining
rep	repeat(ing)
rnd(s)	round(s)
sk	skip
sl	slip
sp(s)	space(s)
st(s)	stitches
sp(s)	space(s)
st(s)	stitch(es)
tog	together
YO	yarn over

* An asterisk (or double asterisks**) in a pattern row, indicates a portion of instructions to be used more than once. For instance, "rep from* three times" means that after working the instructions once, you must work them again three times for a total of 4 times in all.

† A dagger (or double daggers††) indicates those instructions that will be repeated again later in the same row or round.

: The number after a colon tells you the number of stiches you will have when you have completed the row or round.

( ) Parentheses enclose instructions which are to be worked the number of times following the parentheses. For instance, "(ch1, sc,ch 1) 3 times" means that you will chain one, work one sc, and then chain once again three times for a total of six chains and 3sc.

Parentheses often set off or clarify a group of stitches to be worked into the same space or stitch. For instance, "(dc,ch2,dc) in corner sp."

[ ] Brackets and ( ) parentheses are also used to give you additional information.

TERMS

FRONT LOOP—This is the loop toward you at the top of the stitch

BACK LOOP—This is the loop away from you at the top of the stitch

POST—This is the vertical part of the stitch

JOIN—This means to join with a sl st unless another stitch is specified.

FINISH OFF—This means to end your piece by pulling the yarn through the last loop remaining on the hook. This will prevent the work from unraveling.

WORK EVEN—This means that the work is continued in the pattern as established without increasing or decreasing.

TERMS continued next page

TERMS *continued*

CONTINUE IN PATTERN AS ESTABLISHED—This means to follow the pattern stitch as it has been set up, working any increases or decreases in such a way that the pattern remains the same as it was established.

GAUGE

It is extremely important that your personal gauge matches the gauge given in the pattern. Otherwise you may not have enough yarn to complete your afghan. Crochet a swatch that is about 4" square, using the suggested hook and number of stitches given in the pattern. Measure your swatch. If the number of stitches are fewer than those listed in the pattern, try making another swatch with a smaller hook. If the number of stitches are more than are called for in the pattern, try making another swatch with a larger hook.

The afghan patterns in this book have been written using the crochet terminology that is used in the United States. Terms which may have different equivalents in other parts of the world are listed below

United States	**International**
Slip stitch (sl st)	single crochet (sc)
Single crochet (sc)	double crochet (dc)
Half double crochet (hdc)	half treble crochet (htr)
Double crochet (dc)	treble crochet (tr)
Triple crochet (trc)	double treble crochet (dtr)
Double triple crochet (dtr)	triple treble crochet (ttr)
Triple treble crochet (tr tr)	quadruple treble crochet (qtr)
Skip	miss
Gauge	tension
Yarn over (YO)	Yarn over hook (YOH)

CROCHET HOOKS

US	B-1	C-2	D-3	E-4	F-5	G-6	H-8	I-9	J-10	K-10½	N	P	Q
METRIC	2.25	2.75	3.25	3.5	3.75	4	5	5.5	6	6.5	9	10	15

FRINGE

BASIC INSTRUCTIONS

Cut a piece of cardboard about 6" wide and half as long as specified in the instructions for strands, plus 1/2" for trimming allowance. Wind the yarn loosely and evenly lengthwise around cardboard. When the card is filled, cut the yarn across one end. Do this several times; then begin fringing. You can wind additional strands as you need them.

SINGLE KNOT FRINGE

Hold the specified number of strands for one knot of fringe together, then fold in half.

Hold the knitted project with the right side facing you. Using a crochet hook, draw the folded ends through the space or stitch from right to wrong side.

Pull the loose ends through the folded section.

Draw the knot up firmly.

Space the knots as indicated in the pattern instructions. Trim the ends of the fringe evenly.

DOUBLE KNOT FRINGE

Begin by working Single Knot Fringe. With right side facing you and working from left to right, take half the strands of one knot and half the strands in the knot next to it, and knot them together.

Bubble Gum

SIZE: 34" x 42"

MATERIALS

WORSTED WEIGHT YARN: One pound
(16 oz) pink

*Note: Photographed model was made with Lion
Brand Pound of Love, Color #102 Bubble Gum*

Size H (5mm) crochet hook, or size required
for gauge

GAUGE: 4 sc = 1"

INSTRUCTIONS

Ch 146.

ROW 1 (RIGHT SIDE): Sc in 2nd ch from
hook and in each rem ch: 145 sc. Ch 1, turn.

ROW 2: Sc in first sc; * ch 4, sk next 3 sc, sc in
next sc; rep from * across. Ch 1, turn.

ROW 3: Sc in first sc; * ch 4, sk next ch -4 lp,
sc in next sc; rep from * across. Ch 1, turn.

Rep Row 3 until piece measures about 34"
ending by working a wrong side row.

LAST ROW: Sc in first sc; * 3 sc in next ch-4
sp; sc in next sc; rep from * across to last sc, 3
sc in last sc (corner made).

EDGING

RND 1: Turn work so side is at top; ch 4, *sk 3
rows, sc in next row, ch 4; rep from * to corner,
3 sc in corner; turn so beg ch is at top; working in
unused lps of beg ch, ch 4, *sk 3 chs, sc in next
ch, ch 4; rep from *to corner, 3 sc in corner; turn
work so last side is at top; ch 4, *sk 3 rows, sc
in next row, ch 4; rep from *to corner, 3 sc in
corner; turn work so that last row is at top, ch 4,
*sk 3 sc, sc in next sc, ch 4; rep from * across, join
in beg sc, slip st in next sc, ch 1, sc in same sc.

RND 2: *1 sc in ch 4 sp, sc in next sc; rep
from * around, working 3 sc in center sc of each
corner 3-sc group.

Join, finish off; weave in ends.

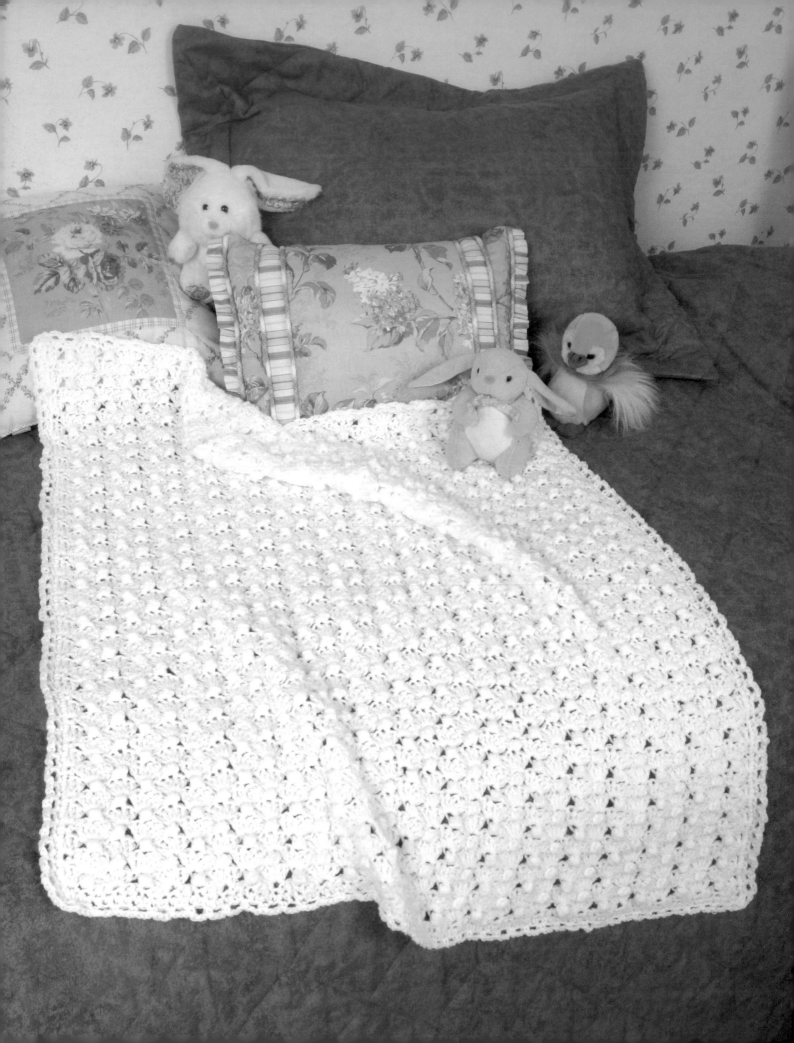

Little Snowballs

SIZE: 37" x 37"

MATERIALS

WORSTED WEIGHT YARN: One pound
(16 oz) white

*Note: Photographed model was made with Lion
Brand Pound of Love, Color #100 White*

Size H (5 mm) crochet hook, or size required
for gauge

GAUGE: 6 sc = 2"

SPECIAL STITCHES

FRONT POPCORN (FPC): 4 sc in designated
st, remove hook from lp and insert from front
to back in first sc of 4-sc group just made; hook
dropped lp and draw through st, ch 1: FPC
made. This is worked on a right-side row.

BACK POPCORN (BPC): 4 sc in designated st,
remove hook from lp and insert from back to
front in first sc of 4-sc group just made; hook
dropped lp and draw through st, ch 1: BPC
made. This is worked on a wrong side row.

INSTRUCTIONS

Loosely ch 98.

ROW 1 (WRONG SIDE): Sc in 2nd ch from
hook and in each rem ch: 97 sc; ch 3, turn.

ROW 2: 2 dc in first sc, sk 2 sc, FPC in next sc;
*sk next 2 sc, 5 dc in next sc (shell made), sk 2
sc, FPC in next sc; rep from * to last 3 sc, sk
next 2 sc, 3 dc in last sc; ch 1, turn.

ROW 3: Sc in first dc, 5-dc shell in ch-1 at top
of next FPC; *BPC in center dc of next 5-dc
shell; 5-dc shell in ch-1 at top of next FPC; rep
from * to last 3 sts, sk 2 dc, sc in top of ch-3.
Ch 3, turn.

ROW 4: 2 dc in first sc; FPC in center dc of
next shell; * 5-dc shell in ch-1 at top of next
BPC, FPC in center dc of next shell; rep from
* across to last sc, 3 dc in last sc. Ch 1, turn.

Rep Rows 3 and 4 until piece measures about
36" long, ending by working a Row 4; at end of
last row, do not ch 1, work sc evenly spaced
around entire afghan, working 3 sc in each
outer corner; join.

EDGING: *Ch 3, sk next sc, sc in next sc; rep
from * around, join. Finish off, weave in ends.

Sweet Lavender

SIZE: 30" x 30"

MATERIALS

WORSTED WEIGHT YARN: One pound
(16 oz) lavender

*Note: Photographed model was made with Lion
Brand Pound of Love, Color #144 Lavender*

Size I (5.5mm) crochet hook, or size required
for gauge

GAUGE: one square = 6"

INSTRUCTIONS

SQUARE (make 16)
Ch 4, join to form a ring.

RND 1 (RIGHT SIDE): Ch 3 (counts as first
dc of rnd), 23 dc in ring; join in 3rd ch of beg
ch-3: 24 dc.

RND 2: Ch 6 (counts as first dc and ch-3 sp),
dc in joining: first corner made; * (ch 1, sk
next dc, dc in next dc) twice; ch 1, sk next dc,
in next dc work (dc, ch 3, dc): corner made;
rep from * twice; (ch 1, sk next dc, dc in next
dc) twice; ch 1, sk next dc; join in 3rd ch of
beg ch-6.

RND 3: Sl st in next ch-3 sp; in same sp work
(ch 3, 3 dc, ch 4, 4 dc); * sk next ch-1 sp, in
next ch-1 sp work (dc, ch 3, dc); sk next ch-1
sp, in next corner ch-3 sp work (4 dc, ch 4, 4
dc); rep from * twice; sk next ch-1 sp, (dc, ch
3, dc) in next ch-1 sp; sk next ch-1 sp; join in
3rd ch of beg ch-3.

RND 4: Ch 3, dc in each of next 3 dc; * in next
corner ch-4 sp work (4 dc, ch 2, 4 dc); dc in
next 4 dc, 3 dc in next ch-3 sp; sk next dc, dc
in next 4 dc; rep from * twice; in next corner
ch-4 sp work (4 dc, ch 2, 4 dc); dc in next 4 dc;
3 dc in next ch-3 sp; join in 3rd ch of beg ch-3.

instructions continued on page 32

Fabulous Fans

SIZE: 50" x 54" before fringing

MATERIALS

WORSTED WEIGHT YARN: Two pounds (32 oz) rose

Note: Photographed model was made with Caron® One Pound, Color #568 Victorian Rose

Size K (6.5mm) crochet hook, or size required for gauge

GAUGE: 16 dc = 6 1/2"

INSTRUCTIONS

Loosely ch 136.

ROW 1: Sc in 2nd ch from hook and in each rem ch: 135 sc. Ch 3, turn (turning ch counts as first st of next row throughout).

ROW 2: Dc in each of next 3 sc; *sk 3 sc, shell of (4 dc, ch 1, 4 dc) all in next st; sk 3 sc , dc in next 8 sc; rep from *across to last 11 sc, sk 3 sc, shell in next sc, sk 3 sc, dc in last 4 sc. Ch 3, turn.

ROW 3: Dc in each of next 3 dc; *ch 4, skip first 4 dc of next shell, sc into ch-1 sp of shell, ch 4, sk next 4 dc of shell, dc in next 8 dc; rep from * across, ending last rep with 4 dc instead of 8 dc. Ch 3, turn.

ROW 4: Dc in next 3 dc; * shell in next sc, dc in next 8 dc; rep from * across, ending by working 4 dc instead of 8 dc. Ch 3, turn.

Rep Rows 3 and 4 for pattern. Work in pattern until piece measures 54", ending by working a Row 4; ch 1, turn.

LAST ROW: Sc in 4 dc; * ch 3, sc in ch-1 sp of next shell; ch 3, sc in next 8 dc; rep from * across, ending with 4 sc. Finish off. Weave in ends.

FRINGE

Follow Single Knot Fringe Instructions on page 5. Cut strands 16" long and use 6 strands for each knot. Knot in center ch-1 sp of each shell group across each short end.

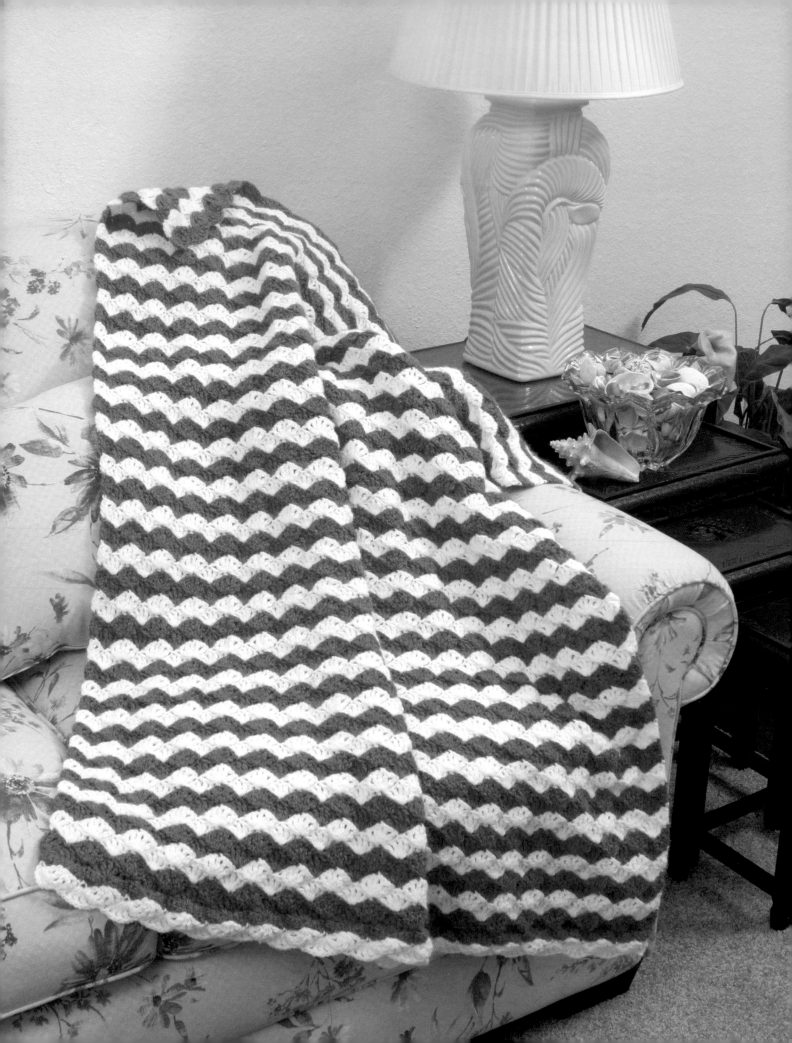

Striped Shells

SIZE: 39" x 50"

MATERIALS

WORSTED WEIGHT YARN: One pound (16 oz) each white (Color A), and blue (Color B)

Note: Photographed model was made with Lion Brand Pound of Love, Color #100 White (A), and Color #110 Denim (B)

Size H (5mm) crochet hook or size required for gauge

GAUGE: 8 dc = 2"; 2 shells = 4"

INSTRUCTIONS

With Color A, ch 162.

ROW 1: Sc in 2nd ch from hook and in each rem ch: 161 sc. Ch 1, turn.

ROW 2: Sc in first sc; *sk 3 sc, in next sc work (tr, ch 1) 4 times, tr in same sc: shell made; sk 3 sc, sc in next sc; rep from * across , ending with sc in last sc: 20 shells. Turn.

ROW 3: Ch 5 (counts as a tr and ch 1), in same sc work (tr, ch 1, tr): half shell made; * sc in center tr of next shell, in next sc work (tr, ch 1) 4 times, tr in same sc; rep from * across,

ending (tr, ch 1) twice, tr in same st: half shell made: 19 shells and 2 half shells. Finish off Color A, turn.

ROW 4: Join Color B with a sc in first tr; * shell in next sc, sc in center tr of next shell; rep from * across, end with sc in 3rd ch of last tr of ending half shell, turn.

ROW 5: Continuing with Color B, rep Row 3. Finish off Color B, turn.

ROWS 6 AND 7: With Color A, rep Rows 4 and 5. Finish off Color A, turn.

Alternating two rows of each color, continue in pattern until piece measures about 50". Finish off.

FINISHING: Hold afghan with beginning ch at top. Join Color B and work Row 2 across, working in unused lps of beg ch. Finish off, weave in ends.

Lovely Lilacs

SIZE: 38" x 53" before fringing

MATERIALS

WORSTED WEIGHT YARN: Two pounds
(32 oz) lilac

*Note: Photographed model was made with Caron®
One Pound, Color #577 Lilac*

Size K (6.5 mm) aluminum crochet hook
(or size required for gauge)

GAUGE: 2 dc and 2 picots = 3"; 2 rows = 1"

INSTRUCTIONS
Chain 118 sts LOOSELY.

ROW 1 (WRONG SIDE): Sc in 6th ch from hook;
* ch 3, sc in first st of ch-3 (picot made); sc in
next ch; ch 2, skip 2 chs, sc next chain. Rep
from * across, ch 3, turn.

ROW 2: 2 Dc in ch-2 space of previous
row; * ch 2, 3 dc into next ch-2 space; rep from
* across, ch 3, turn.

ROW 3: * In next ch 2 sp work (sc, picot, sc),
ch 2; rep from * across, ending with 1 sc after
2nd last dc of previous row; ch 3, turn.

Repeat Rows 2 and 3 until piece measures
about 53", ending by working a Row3. Finish
off, weave in all loose ends.

FRINGE
Follow Single Knot Fringe Instructions on page
5. Cut 174 strands for each side, 16" long. Use
six strands, folded in half, for each knot and tie
knot around the ch-2 bars across each short
end of afghan: 29 knots.

Trim fringe evenly.

Triple Treat Afghan

Size: 48" x 60"

MATERIALS

WORSTED WEIGHT YARN: One pound (16oz) each lilac (Color A), white (Color B), and rose (Color C)

Note: Photographed model was made with Caron® One Pound, Color #577 Lilac (A), Color #501 Bright White (B), and Color #517 Rose (C)

Crochet hook size I (5.5mm) or size required for gauge

GAUGE: 6 dc = 2"

PATTERN STITCH

FRONT POST DOUBLE TRIPLE CROCHET (FPDTR): YO 3 times, insert hook from front to back to front around post of next dc on 2nd row below; draw up a lp, (YO, draw through 2 lps on hook) 4 times: FPdtr made.

Note: Sk dc behind FPdtr.

To change colors: Work last st until 2 lps rem on hook, draw new color through, cut previous color.

INSTRUCTIONS

With Color A, ch 196.

ROW 1 (RIGHT SIDE): Dc in 3rd ch from hook (2 skipped chs count as a dc) and in each rem ch: 194 dc. Ch 2 (counts as first dc on following rows), turn.

instructions continued on next page

Triple Treat Afghan

ROW 2: Dc in each dc, changing to Color B in last st. Cut Color A, ch 2, turn.

ROW 3: Dc in next 4 dc; *FPdtr (see pattern stitch note) around each of next 5 dc on 2nd row below; on working row, dc in next 15 dc; rep from * to last 10 sts; FPdtr around each of next 5 dc on 2nd row below; dc in last 5 dc. Ch 2, turn.

ROW 4: Dc in each st, changing to Color C in last st. Cut Color B, ch 2, turn.

ROW 5: Dc in next 14 dc; *FPdtr around each of next 5 dc on 2nd row below; on working row, dc in next 15 dc; rep from * across.

ROW 6: Rep Row 4.

Working in following color sequence, rep rows 3 through 6 until piece measures 48".

2 rows Color A

2 rows Color B

2 rows Color C

At end of last row, do not ch or turn, finish off. Weave in ends.

FINISHING: With right side facing, join Color B in any outer corner sp. Work sc around all four sides, working 3 sc in corners. Adjust sts as needed to keep work flat.

Daisy Garden

SIZE: 41" x 50"

MATERIALS

WORSTED WEIGHT YARN: One pound (16 oz) each dark rose (Color A), medium rose (Color B), and off white (Color C)

Note: Photographed model was made with Caron® One Pound, Color #535 Country Rose (A), Color #517 Rose (B), and Color #514 Off White (C)

Size H (5 mm) crochet hook, or size required for gauge.

GAUGE: 4 dc = 1"

SPECIAL STITCH

CLUSTER (CL): Keeping last lp of each dc on hook, 2 dc in st indicated; YO and draw through all 3 lps on hook: CL made.

COLOR SEQUENCE: Work colors in sequence: *A, B, C; rep from * to specified length.

INSTRUCTIONS

With Color A, ch 179.

ROW 1 (RIGHT SIDE): Sc in 2nd ch from hook, ch 1, sk next ch, sc in next ch; (ch 3, sk next 3 chs, sc in next ch) twice; *ch 2, sk next 2 chs, sc in next ch; (ch 3, sk next 3 chs, sc in next ch) twice; rep from * to last 2 chs; ch 1, sk next ch, sc in last ch. Ch 2, turn.

instructions continued on page 23

21

ROW 2: In next ch-l sp work [CL (See Pattern St), ch2, CL]; ch 1, sk next ch-3 sp, sc in next sc; *ch 1, sk next ch-3 sp, in next ch-2 sp work (CL, ch 2) 3 times; CL in same sp; ch 1, sk next ch-3 sp, sc in next sc; rep from * to last ch-3 sp; ch 1, sk last ch-3 sp, in next ch-1 sp work (CL, ch2, CL); dc in next sc; change to next color by drawing lp through; cut first color. Ch 1, turn.

ROW 3: Sc in first dc; *ch 3, CL in top of each of next 4 Cls; ch 3, sc in next ch-2 sp; rep from * across, working last sc in 2nd ch of turning ch-2. Ch 1, turn.

ROW 4: Sc in first sc; *ch 3, sc in top of next CL, ch 2, sk next 2 Cls, sc in top of next CL, ch 3, sc in next sc; rep from * across. Ch 1, turn.

ROW 5: Sc in first sc; *ch 1, sk next ch-3 sp, in next ch-2 sp work (CL, ch 2) 3 times; CL in same sp; ch 1, sk next ch-3 sp, sc in next sc; rep from * across; change to next color; cut old color. Ch 2, turn.

ROW 6: CL in top of each of next 2 CLs; ch 3, sc in next ch-2 sp, ch 3; *CL in top of each of next 4 CLs; ch 3, sc in next ch-2 sp, ch 3; rep from * to last 2 CLs; CL in top of each of last 2 CLs; dc in last sc. Ch 1, turn.

ROW 7: Sc in first dc, ch 1, sk next CL, sc in next CL, ch 3, sc in next sc, ch 3; *sc in top of next CL, ch 2, sk next 2 CLs, sc in top of next CL, ch 3, sc in next sc, ch 3; rep from * to last 2 CLs; sc in next CL, ch 1, sk last CL, sc in 2nd ch of turning ch-2. Ch 2, turn.

ROW 8: In next ch-1 sp work (CL, ch2, CL); ch 1, sk next ch-3 sp, sc in next sc; *ch 1, sk next ch-3 sp, in next ch-2 sp work (CL, ch 2) 3 times; CL in same sp; ch 1, sk next ch-3 sp, sc in next sc; rep from * to last ch-3 sp; ch 1, sk last ch-3 sp, in next ch-1 sp work (CL, ch2, CL); dc in next sc; change to next color, cut old color. Ch 1, turn.

Rep Rows 3 through 8 for desired length, ending with Row 7. At end of last row, do not ch 2; do not turn.

Finish off, weave in ends.

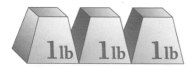

Fisherman Shells

Size: 40" x 60"

MATERIALS

WORSTED WEIGHT YARN: Three pounds (48 oz) off white

Note: Photographed model was made with Red Heart® Giant Pounder, Color #2082 Aran

Size H (5mm) crochet hook, or size required for gauge

GAUGE: 7 sc = 2" 6 rows sc = 1 1/2"

Note: To work shell: Insert hook from front to back to front around vertical stem of specified dc; work shell of (sc, hdc, 3 dc) around stem.

INSTRUCTIONS
(Pattern is worked vertically)
Ch 211.

ROW 1: Sc in 2nd ch from hook and in each rem ch: 210 sc. Ch 1, turn.

ROWS 2 THROUGH 5: Sc in each sc. Ch 1, turn.

ROW 6: Sc in each sc. Ch 3, turn.

ROW 7: Dc in each sc, turn.

ROW 8: (RIGHT SIDE): Ch 3 (counts as first dc of row), sc in next dc, work shell around stem of same dc; *sk 2 dc, sc in next dc, shell around stem of same dc; rep from * across, dc in last dc; ch 1, turn.

ROW 9: Sc in each skipped dc and in each sc; ch 1, turn.

ROWS 10 THROUGH 13: Sc in each sc, ch 1, turn.

ROW 14: Sc in each sc, ch 3, turn.

Rep Rows 7 through 14 for pattern until piece measures about 40", ending by working a Row 14. Finish off, weave in ends.

FRINGE
Cut remaining yarn into 22" long strands.

Following Single Knot Fringe instructions on page 5, tie knots across each end, using 4 strands in each shell row knot and one strand in all other rows. Trim fringe evenly.

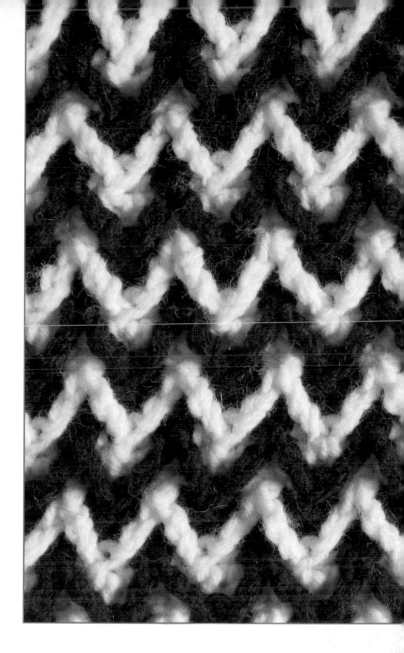

Arrowheads

SIZE: 48" x 52"

MATERIALS

WORSTED WEIGHT YARN: Two pounds
(32 oz) each black (Color A) and white
(Color B)

*Note: Photographed model was made with Red
Heart® Giant Pounder, Color #2094 Black (A) and
Color #2081 White (B)*

Size H (5 mm) crochet hook or size required
for gauge

GAUGE: 4 sc = 1"

TO CHANGE COLORS: Work stitch up to last
step, work off last step with new color; do not
cut previous color; carry color not in use loosely up side.

SPECIAL STITCH

TR2TOG 3 ROWS BELOW: Work 1 tr into
same st as last tr until last lp of tr remains on
hook, skip 3 sts, work 1 tr into next skipped st
3 rows below until last lp of tr remains on
hook, YO and through all 3 lps.

*Note: Sts on either side of tr2tog must be worked
behind tr2tog.*

INSTRUCTIONS

With Color A, ch 196,

ROW 1 (RIGHT SIDE): Sc in 2nd ch from
hook and in next 2 ch; * ch 1, skip next ch, sc
in each of next 3 ch; rep from * across, turn.

ROW 2: Ch 3 (counts as first dc of row), skip
first sc, dc in each st across (working into actu-
al st of each ch, not into ch sp) to last st, dc in
last st, changing to Color B, turn.

instructions continued on next page

Arrowheads

ROW 3: Ch 1, sc in first dc, tr into first skipped starting ch, skip 1 dc on 2nd row, sc into next dc, ch 1, skip 1 dc, sc into next dc, *tr2tog 3 rows below (into skipped starting ch) skip 1 dc on 2nd row, sc into next dc, ch 1, skip 1 dc, sc into next dc; rep from * to last 2 dc, tr into same ch as 2nd leg of last tr2tog, skip 1 dc, sc into 3rd ch of ch 3 at beg of previous row, turn.

ROW 4: Ch 3, skip first sc, dc in each st across, change to Color A in last st; turn.

ROW 5: Ch 1, sc in first dc, tr into next skipped dc 3 rows below, skip 1 dc on previous row, sc into next dc, ch 1, skip 1 dc, sc into next dc, *tr2tog 3 rows below, skip 1 dc on previous row, sc into next dc, ch 1, skip 1 dc, sc into next dc; rep from * to last 2 dc, 1 tr into same dc as 2nd leg of last tr2tog, skip 1 dc, sc into 3rd ch of ch 3 at beg of previous row, turn.

ROW 6: Rep Row 4, using Color A instead of Color B.

ROW 7: Rep Row 5, using Color B instead of Color A.

Rep Rows 4-7 until piece measures about 52", ending by working a Row 7.

Finish off, weave in ends.

Mosaic

SIZE: 46" x 60"

MATERIALS

WORSTED WEIGHT YARN: Two pounds
(32 oz) each cream (Color A) beige (Color B)

*Note: Photographed model was made with
Caron® One Pound, Color #589 Cream (A),
and Color #585 Lace (B).*

Size H (5mm) crochet hook, or size required
for gauge

GAUGE: 7 sts = 2"

*Note: To change colors, work first color until one
step remains in last stitch, finish last stitch with
new color.*

INSTRUCTIONS

With Color A, ch 167.

ROW 1: Sc in 2nd ch from
hook and in each rem ch: 166 sc. Ch 1, turn.

ROW 2 (RIGHT SIDE): Sc in each sc across,
changing to Color B in last sc. Ch 3 (counts as
dc on following rows), turn. Finish off cream.

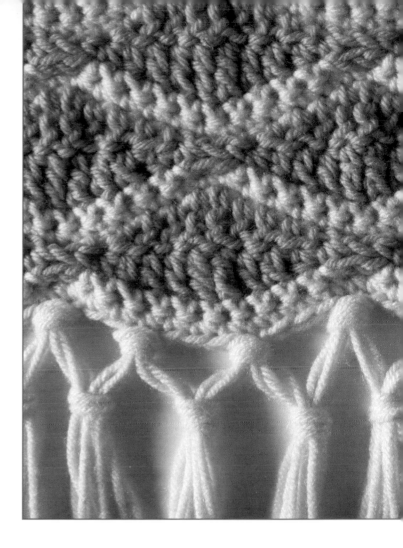

ROW 3: Dc in next sc, hdc in next sc, sc in
next sc; * ch 2, sk next 2 sc, sc in next sc, hdc
in next sc, dc in next 2 sc, trc in next 2 sc, dc
in next 2 sc, hdc in next sc, sc in next sc; rep
from * 12 times more; ch 2, sk next 2 sc, sc
in next sc, hdc in next sc, dc in next 2 sc.
Ch 3, turn.

ROW 4: Dc in next dc, hdc in next hdc, sc in
next sc; * ch 2, sk next ch-2 sp, sc in next sc,
hdc in next hdc, dc in next 2 dc, trc in next 2
trc, dc in next 2 dc, hdc in next hdc, sc in next
sc; rep from * 12 times more; ch 2, sk next ch-2
sp, sc in next sc, hdc in next hdc, dc in next dc
and in 3rd ch of turning ch-3, changing to
Color A in last dc. Ch 1, turn.
Finish off Color B.

instructions continued on page 31

ROW 5: Sc in first 4 sts; working in front of work, sc in each of next 2 skipped sc on 3rd row below; * on working row sc in next 10 sts, working in front of work, sc in each of next 2 skipped sc on 3rd row below; rep from * to last 4 sts, sc in each of next 3 sts and in 3rd ch of turning ch-3. Ch 1, turn.

ROW 6: Sc in each sc; changing to Color B in last sc. Ch 1, turn. Finish off Color A.

ROW 7: Sc in first sc, hdc in next sc, dc in next 2 sc, trc in next 2 sc, dc in next 2 sc, hdc in next sc, sc in next sc; * ch 2, sk next 2 sc, sc in next sc, hdc in next sc, dc in next 2 sc, trc in next 2 sc, dc in next 2 sc, hdc in next sc, sc in next sc; rep from across. Ch 1, turn.

ROW 8: Sc in first sc, hdc in next hdc, dc in next 2 dc, trc in next 2 trc, dc in next 2 dc, hdc in next hdc, sc in next sc; * ch 2, sk next ch-2, sc in next sc, hdc in next hdc, dc in next 2 dc, trc in next 2 trc, dc in next 2 dc, hdc in next hdc, sc in next sc; rep from * across; changing to Color A in last sc. Ch 1, turn. Finish off Color B.

ROW 9: Sc in first 10 sts; * working in front of work, sc in each of next 2 skipped sc on 3rd row below; on working row, sc in next 10 sts; rep from * across. Ch 1, turn.

Rep Rows 2 through 9 until afghan measures about 60". Work Row 2 once more. Finish off, weave in ends.

FRINGE

Follow Double Knot Fringe Instructions on page 5. Using Color A cut stands 20" long and use 4 strands in each knot. Tie knot through every fourth stitch across short ends of afghan.

Sweet Lavender *continued from page 11*

RND 5: Ch 1; * sc in each dc to ch-2 sp; 3 sc in next ch-2 sp; rep from * 3 times more; sc in each rem dc; join in first sc.

RND 6: Ch 1; * sc in each sc to center sc of next 3 sc group, 3 sc in center sc; rep from * 3 times more; sc in each rem sc; join in first sc. Finish off and weave in all ends.

ASSEMBLY

To join, hold two squares with right sides tog and sew through back loops only. Join in four rows of four squares each, carefully matching corners.

RUFFLE

RND 1: Join yarn in center sc of 3-sc group in any outer corner; in same st work (ch 3, dc, ch 2, 2 dc) for beg corner; * hdc in each st and each joining to next corner 3-sc group; in center sc work (2 dc, ch 2, 2 dc); rep from * twice, hdc in each rem st and joining, join in 3rd ch of beg ch-3.

RND 2: Sl st in next dc and into ch-2 sp; (ch 3, dc, ch 2, 2 dc) all in same sp; sk next 2 dc; *in next hdc work (dc, ch 1, dc); sk next hdc; rep from * to next corner, in corner ch-2 sp work (dc, ch 2, dc); sk next 2 dc; rep from * twice; ** sk next hdc, (dc, ch 1,dc) in next hdc; rep from ** to beg corner, join in 3rd ch of beg ch-3.

RND 3: Sl st in next dc and into ch-2 sp; in same sp work (ch 3, 2 dc, ch 2, 3 dc); * 3 dc in each ch-1 sp to next corner; in corner ch-2 sp work (3 dc, ch 2, 3 dc); rep from * twice, 3 dc in each rem ch-1 sp, join in third ch of beg ch 3.

RND 4: Ch 3, sk next dc, sc in next dc; ch 4, sc in next dc, ch 3, sk next dc, sc in next dc: beg corner made; *sc in next dc, ch 3, sk next dc, sc in next dc; rep from * to next corner; ch 4, sk ch-3 sp; rep from * twice, **sc in next dc, ch 3, sk next dc; rep from *, join to 3rd ch of beg ch-3. Finish off, weave in ends.